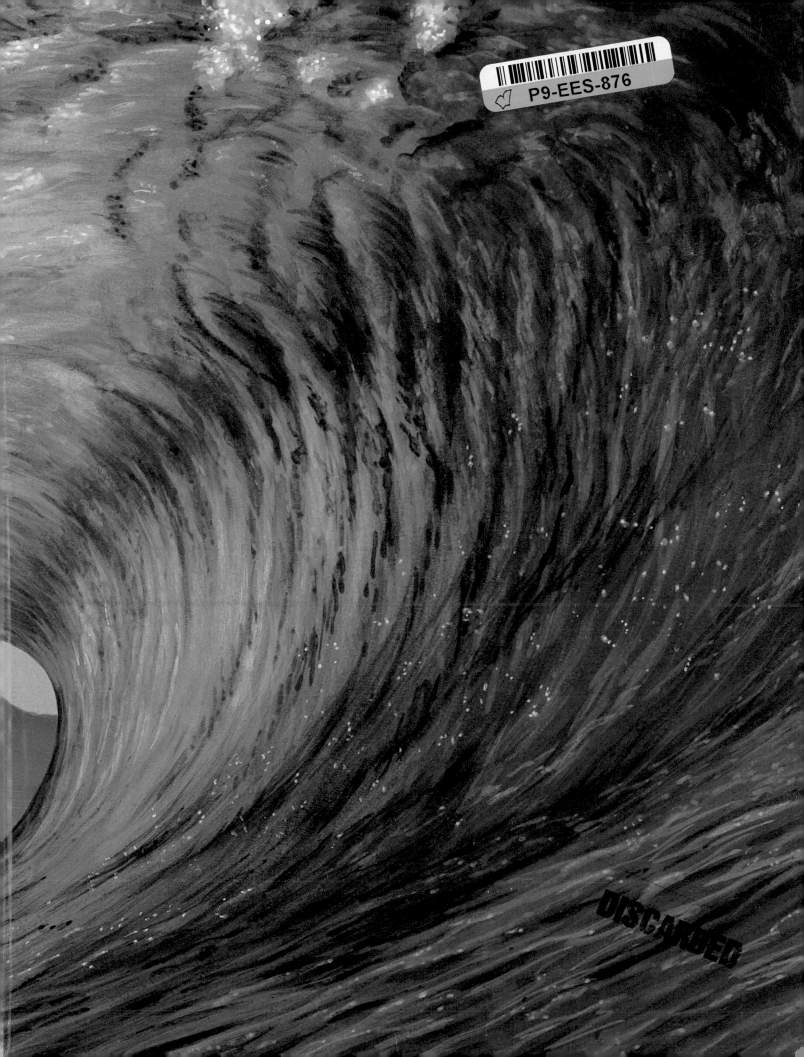

P9-EES-876

DISCARDED

The Seven Seas

EXPLORING THE WORLD OCEAN

Linda Vieira

Illustrations by Higgins Bond

Walker & Company
New York

Lake Agassiz Regional Library
118 S. 5th St. P.O. Box 900
Moorhead, MN 56560

Copyright © 2003 by Linda Vieira
Illustrations copyright © 2003 by Higgins Bond

All rights reserved. No part of this book may be reproduced or
transmitted in any form or by any means, electronic or mechanical,
including photocopying, recording, or by any information storage
and retrieval system, without permission in writing from the
Publisher.

First published in the United States of America in 2003 by
Walker Publishing Company, Inc.

Published simultaneously in Canada by Fitzhenry and Whiteside,
Markham, Ontario L3R 4T8

For information about permission to reproduce selections from
this book, write to Permissions, Walker & Company, 435 Hudson Street,
New York, New York 10014

Library of Congress Cataloging-in-Publication Data
available upon request
ISBN 0-8027-8833-5 (hardcover)
ISBN 0-8027-8834-3 (reinforced)

The illustrations for this book were done in acrylic on illustration board.

Book design by Victoria Allen

Visit Walker & Company's Web site at www.walkerbooks.com

Printed in Hong Kong

10 9 8 7 6 5 4 3 2 1

This book is dedicated to
Keely Julianne White, Taylor Jordan Tractenberg, and
Lauren Elizabeth Tractenberg, who made me what I am today—Grandmommy.
—L. V.

For Benny.
—H. B.

5,000,000 B.C.E.

CONTINENT

NORTH
AMERICA

EUROPE

ASIA

Arabia

AFRICA

SOUTH
AMERICA

India

Madagascar

AUSTRALIA

ANTARCTICA

NORTH
AMERICA

SOUTH
AMERICA

CONTINENT

MAGMA

The Sea Is Everywhere

Millions of years ago, violent earthquakes buckled and cracked the surface of the Earth, creating elevated landforms and bottomless gorges. The land was constantly changing. It shifted and inched together, forming one supercontinent surrounded by an enormous world ocean.

Then, over time, the land broke apart again and again, spreading out in the watery depths to create six separate continents: North America, South America, Africa, Europe/Asia, Australia, and Antarctica. The world ocean around them came to be known by five different names: Pacific, Atlantic, Indian, Arctic, and Antarctic.

Seas and gulfs are smaller bodies of ocean water, often surrounded by land. Together, the oceans, seas, and gulfs are called "the Seven Seas," and they sustain the largest environment of living things on Earth.

ASIA

EUROPE

India

Arabia

AFRICA

Madagascar

AUSTRALIA

ANTARCTICA

Siberia

BERING
LAND
BRIDGE
(Beringia)

Alaska

CORDILLERAN
ICE SHEET

The Sea Is Shallow

The Arctic Ocean around the North Pole is the smallest ocean. It fills a shallow basin that is about 4,300 feet deep and covers continental shelves, gradual sloping edges of submerged land.

Towering glaciers cover part of the Arctic. As the summer sun thaws the ice, enormous chunks break off and crash into the sea as icebergs.

Billions of algae bloom in the warmed water. Small sea creatures feed on algae, attracting fish. Seals dive for fish, and walruses root out shellfish along the coast. Polar bears and killer whales hunt for seals, and baleen whales strain seawater for tiny shrimplike creatures called krill.

During an ice age about 13,000 years ago, frozen water lowered ocean levels, exposing more than 2 million acres of dry land underneath the Bering Sea. Large animals migrated south looking for food. Early humans followed the animals they hunted across this land bridge and eventually settled in North and South America.

5,000,000 B.C.E.   11,000 B.C.E.   2,500 B.C.E.

MID-PACIFIC MOUNTAINS

HAWAIIAN RIDGE

Mauna Kea

The Sea Is Deep

The Pacific is the largest, deepest ocean, capturing half the Earth's seawater between the Americas and Asia. Earthquakes relentlessly grind and shrink its seafloor, making it smaller. The Challenger Deep, a trench in the Pacific plunging 35,838 feet below sea level, is the deepest point on Earth. Hawaii's Mauna Kea, measuring 31,796 feet from its underwater base to its peak, is the tallest.

In Pacific waters near Australia, an ancient coral garden called the Great Barrier Reef is home to thousands of species of colorful fish. Piled about 500 feet high with skeletons of tiny animals, it spans 1,250 miles and is the largest natural structure on Earth.

About 4,500 years ago, islanders near southeast Asia were driven from their homes by wars or famine. For the next thousand years, they navigated east across an unknown ocean to discover and colonize Polynesia.

They observed star positions and habits of migratory birds, sailing toward greenish reflections of forests that they saw shining on the undersides of distant clouds.

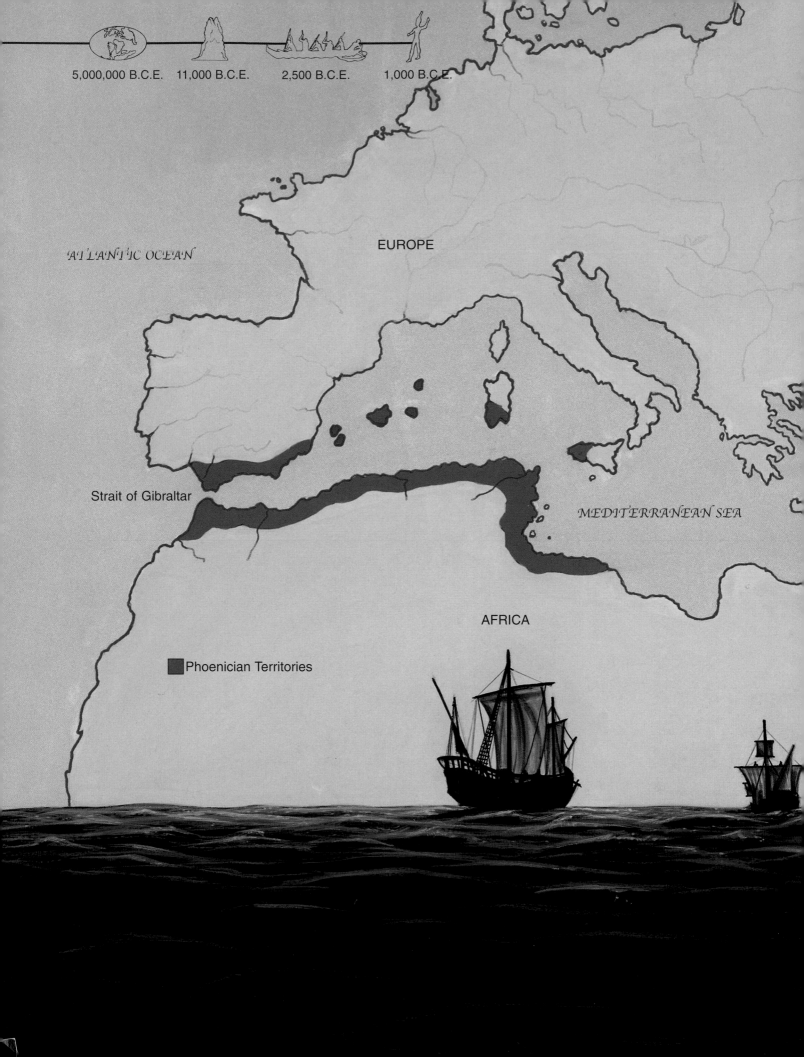

5,000,000 B.C.E.   11,000 B.C.E.   2,500 B.C.E.   1,000 B.C.E.

ATLANTIC OCEAN

EUROPE

Strait of Gibraltar

MEDITERRANEAN SEA

AFRICA

Phoenician Territories

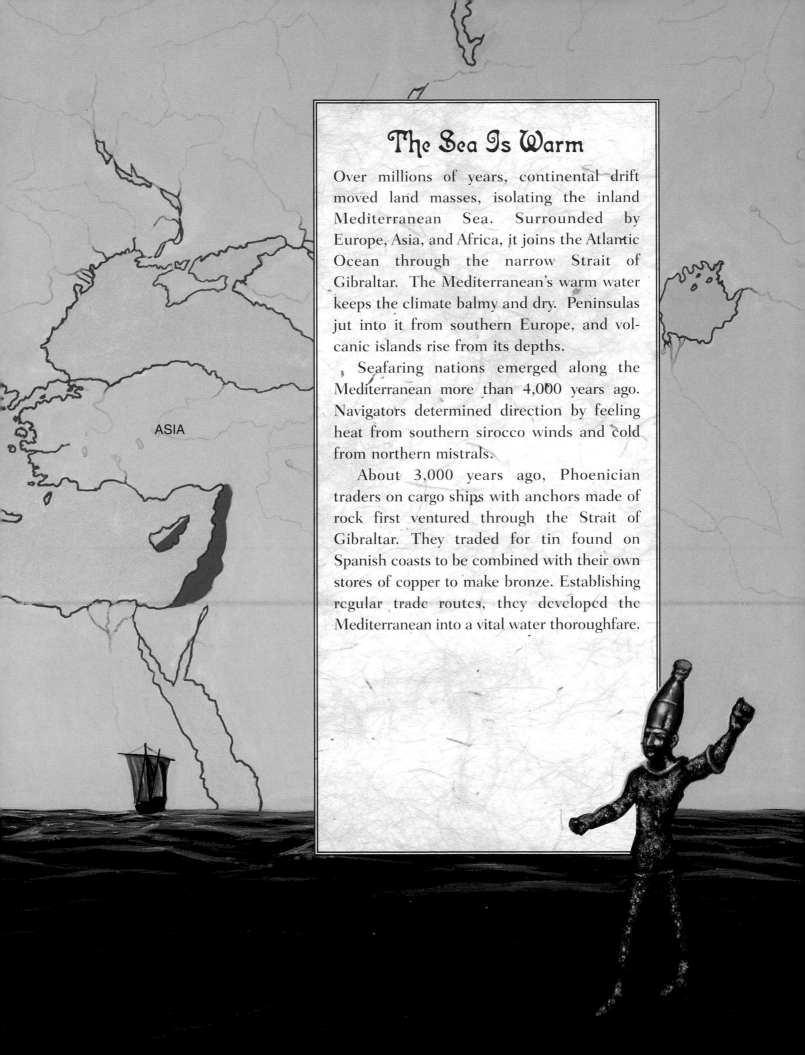

The Sea Is Warm

Over millions of years, continental drift moved land masses, isolating the inland Mediterranean Sea. Surrounded by Europe, Asia, and Africa, it joins the Atlantic Ocean through the narrow Strait of Gibraltar. The Mediterranean's warm water keeps the climate balmy and dry. Peninsulas jut into it from southern Europe, and volcanic islands rise from its depths.

Seafaring nations emerged along the Mediterranean more than 4,000 years ago. Navigators determined direction by feeling heat from southern sirocco winds and cold from northern mistrals.

About 3,000 years ago, Phoenician traders on cargo ships with anchors made of rock first ventured through the Strait of Gibraltar. They traded for tin found on Spanish coasts to be combined with their own stores of copper to make bronze. Establishing regular trade routes, they developed the Mediterranean into a vital water thoroughfare.

ASIA

5,000,000 B.C.E.   11,000 B.C.E.   2,500 B.C.E.   1,000 B.C.E.   999 C.E.

MID-ATLANTIC RIDGE

OCEANIC CRUST

The Sea Is Mountainous

The Atlantic is the second largest ocean, extending east of the Americas and west of Europe and Africa, almost from pole to pole. Undersea volcanoes pile oozing lava onto tall ridges along its seafloor. Continuous plate movements pull the ridges apart, and molten rock rises into the cracks.

These connected ridges under the oceans form the Mid-Atlantic Ridge, the longest mountain range on Earth. This continuously spreading seabed snakes for 7,000 miles, covering nearly the entire ocean floor, from north to south, and is slowly enlarging the Atlantic. In the Denmark Strait, water slowly cascades 2.2 miles over an underwater cliff, Earth's most spectacular waterfall.

Europeans navigated the Atlantic as early as 500 C.E., when Irish monks sailed leather boats to Iceland. Vikings crossed the Atlantic in vessels called knarrs. "Erik the Red" Thorvaldson explored the southern coast of Greenland between 982 and 985 C.E.

Navigating with early instruments, they relied on ancient principles—star positions, patterns of winds and waves, and the sun's height as it arced across the sky.

OCEANIC RIDGE

MAGMA

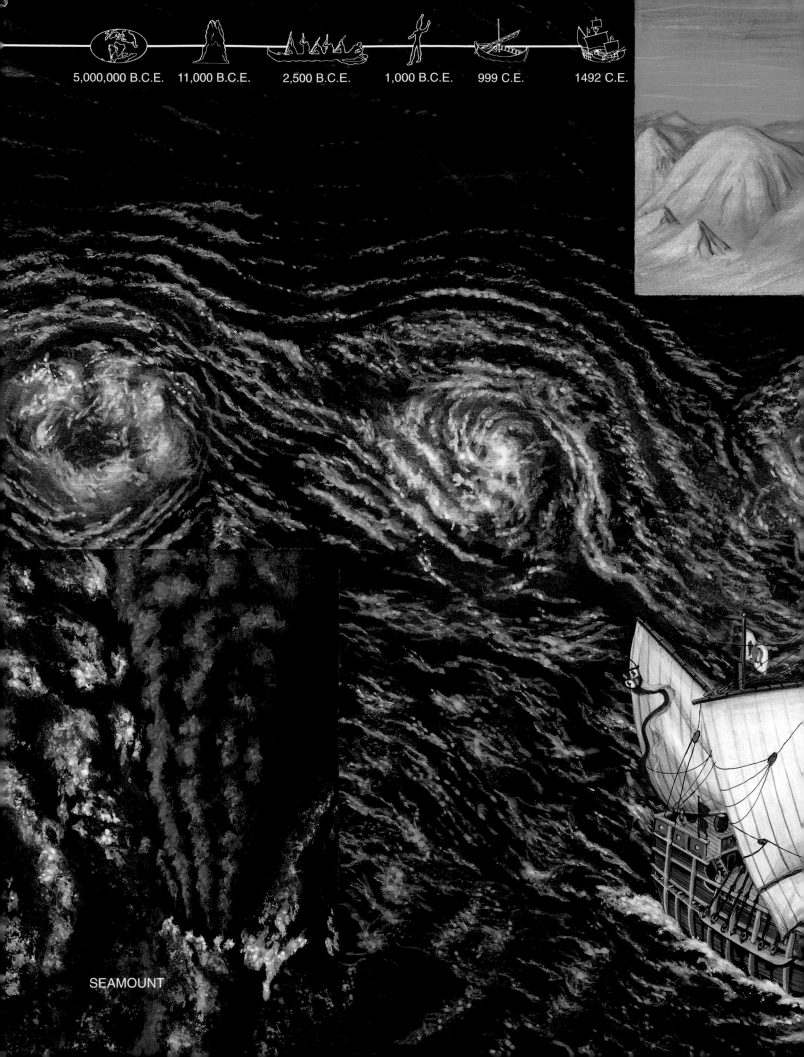

5,000,000 B.C.E.   11,000 B.C.E.   2,500 B.C.E.   1,000 B.C.E.   999 C.E.   1492 C.E.

SEAMOUNT

The Sea Is Moving

The ocean is never still. Waves and tides ripple across its basins, propelled by the gravitational pull of the sun and moon. Ocean waters flow thousands of miles in huge, wavy ribbons called currents.

Wind-driven surface currents spread heat around the Earth by bringing warmed water to continental shores. Deep water currents roll over fiery underwater volcanoes called seamounts. Hot mineral water from inside the Earth gushes into currents through hydrothermal vents in the ocean floor.

European adventurers dreamed of conquering nations and discovering treasures beyond their horizons. They yearned for riches and glory and to know the true size and shape of the world.

Italian trader Marco Polo traveled overland east to China in the late 1200s. Laden with silks and spices, he returned after twenty-four years with amazing tales of wealth in the Far East. Christopher Columbus sailed across the Atlantic in 1492 to find a shorter route to the riches of China, but he discovered an unknown continent—North America—instead.

5,000,000 B.C.E.   11,000 B.C.E.   2,500 B.C.E.   1,000 B.C.E.   999 C.E.   1492 C.E.   1521 C.E.

ASIA

NORTH
AMERICA

EUROPE

*PACIFIC
OCEAN*

Spain

*ATLANTIC
OCEAN*

AFRICA

*INDIAN
OCEAN*

AUSTRALIA

Magellan's Voyage

SOUTH
AMERICA

*Cape
of Good Hope*

*Strait of
Magellan*

The Sea Is Stormy

The Indian Ocean is the third largest ocean, lying between Africa and Australia. Seasonal air over the ocean affects weather patterns in surrounding areas.

In winter, fierce monsoons blow hot and dry from land to sea, leaving behind devastating sandstorms and drought. Summer monsoons bring flooding rains from sea to mainland. Destructive cyclones form over the ocean at any time, driving gale-force winds toward shore.

Adventurers and traders braved dangerous ocean storms in the race to find treasures and discover new lands. In 1487, Portugal's Bartolomeu Dias reached the Indian Ocean. He sailed around Africa's Cape of Good Hope in such bad weather that he did not even see it. In 1521, an oceanic expedition begun by Ferdinand Magellan and plagued by storms as well as mutiny successfully circumnavigated the world.

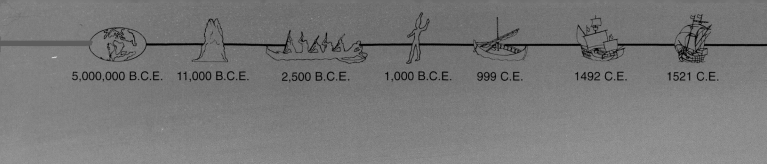

The Sea Is Clear

The vast Gulf of Mexico, where warm Gulf Stream currents begin, is almost completely surrounded by southeastern North America. The crystalline water of the Caribbean Sea, about 1 million square miles between North and South America, is full of reefs and multicolored fish. Spanish galleons, attacked by sixteenth-century pirates, have been discovered there by treasure-seeking divers.

Although crime on the high seas existed long before the time of the Vikings, the seventeenth and eighteenth centuries were the Golden Age of Piracy. Legends glorified the bloody exploits of Captain Kidd, Blackbeard, and Calico Jack, as well as Anne Bonny and Mary Read. According to folklore, the ocean floor is littered with plundered ships and treasures.

5,000,000 B.C.E. 11,000 B.C.E. 2,500 B.C.E. 1,000 B.C.E. 999 C.E. 1492 C.E. 1521 C.E.

The Sea Is Freezing

The Antarctic Ocean, colder and less salty than the others, surrounds the ice-covered continent of Antarctica at the South Pole. Circular winds around this desolate mass of land force its gigantic ocean current northward. The icy floe slides under warmer seawater, pushing it upward in a process called upwelling.

Whales and seals hunt for food among icebergs in the warmer water. Thousands of penguins gather in rookeries on frozen shores to find mates and lay eggs.

Captain James Cook of England was the first to explore the Antarctic in the late eighteenth century. His wooden ship couldn't penetrate the thick, slushy ice, and he did not find land. He was the first captain to prevent scurvy among sailors by providing daily rations of sauerkraut and limes, which contain vitamin C.

By 1800, all surface areas of the world ocean had been explored.

AFRICA

INDIAN OCEAN

AUSTRALIA

PACIFIC OCEAN

Tahiti

Marquesas Is.

SOUTH AMERICA

Cook Is.

Tonga Is.

Easter Is.

ATLANTIC OCEAN

New Zealand

Cook's Voyage

ANTARCTIC OCEAN

ANTARCTICA

5,000,000 B.C.E. 11,000 B.C.E. 2,500 B.C.E. 1,000 B.C.E. 999 C.E. 1492 C.E. 1521 C.E.

MEDITERRANEAN SEA

Israel

Suez Canal

Egypt

Sinai

RED
SEA

Gulf of Mexico — Central America

PACIFIC OCEAN

CARIBBEAN SEA

Panama Canal

SOUTH AMERICA

The Sea Is Busy

Traders continued to search for shorter ocean routes. In 1869, the Suez Canal was built, connecting small lakes between the Mediterranean and Red Seas. It shortened expeditions from England to India by 6,000 miles.

In 1914, the Panama Canal was gouged out of Central American swamps and jungles, linking the Atlantic and Pacific. Called "the Crossroads of the World," it cut the journey from the east coast of North America to the west coast by almost 8,000 miles.

Modern ocean research began in 1872 with England's HMS *Challenger*, which explored 68,000 miles underneath the sea. Along with the USS *Albatross*, it enabled scientists to discover new species of plants and animals.

Many years later, Jacques Cousteau and Emile Gagnan perfected the first self-contained underwater breathing apparatus— or scuba gear—in 1943. Cousteau brought the wonders of the sea to millions of people via television.

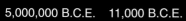 

5,000,000 B.C.E.   11,000 B.C.E.   2,500 B.C.E.   1,000 B.C.E.   999 C.E.   1492 C.E.   1521 C.E.

The Sea Is Topographical

The highest peaks, deepest trenches, and longest mountain ranges on Earth are hidden underwater. They lie in basins on the ocean floor, along with canyons, volcanoes, plateaus, and plains.

Vast abyssal plains in the deepest oceans are the flattest lands on Earth. Strange creatures live there, adapted to the crushing pressures of the sea. Some look like flowers or trees, and others have unhinging jaws, luminous bodies, or walk on stiltlike fins.

The explorations of marine scientist Dr. Robert Ballard found plants that produce food and oxygen through photosynthesis without sunlight. Scientists are studying this phenomenon to determine if life can exist on other planets.

Ballard charted the ocean floor using a remote-controlled photographic robot, camera, and monitor. His expeditions made headlines around the world in 1985 when he located the sunken ship *Titanic*.

5,000,000 B.C.E. 11,000 B.C.E. 2,500 B.C.E. 1,000 B.C.E. 999 C.E. 1492 C.E. 1521 C.E.

The Sea Is Bountiful

Rushing rivers wash particles of every element on Earth into the sea. Large deposits of gas and oil, necessary to fuel the world's machinery, are buried deep in rocky layers beneath the seafloor.

The sea has been a food source for thousands of years and is harvested for other things as well. Sunlight penetrates shallow continental shelves for about 100 feet, allowing green plants to thrive. Marine creatures and fish flock there to eat the plants. Ninety percent of all food fish are caught each year in these shallow waters.

Other products made from ocean compounds are animal food, medicines, varnish, fertilizer, and cosmetics. Today, marine farmers raise fish, shellfish, tiny phytoplankton, and other organisms on underwater farms. Mariculturalists in more than 150 countries are designing systems to meet the needs of Earth's growing population.

5,000,000 B.C.E.   11,000 B.C.E.   2,500 B.C.E.   1,000 B.C.E.   999 C.E.   1492 C.E.   1521 C.E.

The Sea Is in Danger

The ocean is a dumping ground for fertilizers and pesticides washed from land to rivers that empty into the sea. These pollutants are spilled or pumped directly into oceans or fall into the sea with rain, reducing oxygen in seawater. Lack of oxygen kills food-producing marine organisms along the food chain.

Atmospheric gases trap solar heat, reflecting it back to Earth in a greenhouse effect. Global warming from increased heat threatens to melt Arctic and Antarctic ice, raising ocean levels. Low-lying areas of the Earth would be threatened, and almost half the world's population would have to relocate.

Every year, the atmosphere's ozone layer thins out over icy Antarctica. This widening hole in the ozone allows more ultraviolet radiation to threaten marine ecosystems.

5,000,000 B.C.E.   11,000 B.C.E.   2,500 B.C.E.   1,000 B.C.E.   999 C.E.   1492 C.E.   1521 C.E.

The Sea Is Essential

Life exists because of water in the ocean, and the same water has been recycled by solar energy since the Earth was formed. Your teardrops could have once been snowflakes falling on dinosaurs millions of years before you were born.

Seventy-five percent of all solar energy is absorbed by seawater. Before limited oil reserves are used up, scientists want to harness that energy to provide unlimited power in the future.

The ocean is our planet's largest source of food, fuel, and energy. Earth's magnificent sea, the one world ocean, holds the key to life and the betterment of humankind.

Glossary

abyssal plain—vast region of flatland underneath the sea

algae—plantlike marine organisms

basin—shallow underwater crater

circumnavigate—sail around the world without crossing land

continental drift—huge pieces, or plates, of Earth's crust floating on its mantle, moving land masses toward and away from each other

continental shelf—gradual sloping edges of submerged land masses, near continental shores

current—flowing air or water

cyclone—very strong wind and rain moving in a large circular pattern

glacial epoch—period in history when much of Earth was covered by ice

glaciers—slowly moving rivers of ice

hole in the ozone—reduction of the atmospheric gas that reduces harmful solar rays

hydrothermal vent—opening in the ocean floor through which hot mineral water gushes upward

land bridge—ocean floor between Siberia and Alaska, exposed when glacial ice lowered sea levels

mariculturalist—farmer who grows marine plants and animals

mistral—strong, cold north wind blowing across the Mediterranean Sea

monsoon—eastern wind that changes direction seasonally

ocean—continuous body of salt water surrounding Earth's continents and known by different names: Pacific, Atlantic, Indian, Arctic, Antarctic

photosynthesis—production of food and oxygen by green plants in sunlight

reef—piled-up skeletons of tiny coral animals

rookery—where marine animals breed and raise their young

scuba—self-contained underwater breathing apparatus

scurvy—disease caused by vitamin-C deficiency

seamount—fiery underwater volcano

seas and gulfs—smaller bodies of ocean water, mostly surrounded by land

seven seas—all the ocean waters on Earth

sirocco—strong, warm south wind blowing across the Mediterranean Sea

upwelling—warm water forced upward by cold-water current

DL
NO 30 '03

CR
AP 15 '04

HL

JY 15 '04
MH
DC 15 '04

MC

J 551.46 Vie

Vieira, Linda.

The seven seas :
FO 3350007676620